Bees Up Close

Robin Birch

Raintree

Chicago, Illinois

© 2005 Raintree

Published by Raintree, a division of Reed Elsevier, Inc.

Chicago, Illinois

Customer Service 888-363-4266

Visit our website at www.raintreelibrary.com

For information, address the publisher:
Raintree, 100 N. LaSalle, Suite 1200, Chicago, IL 60602

09 08 07 06 05
10 9 8 7 6 5 4 3 2 1

Printed and bound in Hong Kong and China by WKT Company Limited.

Library of Congress Cataloging-in-Publication Data
Birch, Robin.
 Bees up close / Robin Birch.
   p. cm. -- (Minibeasts up close)
 Includes bibliographical references and index.
 ISBN 1-4109-1138-1 -- ISBN 1-4109-1145-4
 1. Bees--Juvenile literature. I. Title. II. Series: Birch, Robin.
Minibeasts up close.
 QL565.2.B57 2004
 595.79'9--dc22

                                    2004003109

Acknowledgments
The publisher would like to thank the following for permission to reproduce photographs:
pp. 4, 15, 21 OSF; p. 5 Jeff Wright/Queensland Museum; pp. 6, 11 Jiri Lochman/Lochman Transparencies; p. 7 Frank Park/ANT Photo Library; pp. 8, 20 Kim Taylor/Bruce Coleman Inc.; pp. 10, 28 photolibrary.com; p. 12 Pascal Goetgheluck/ARDEA London; p. 13 Susumu Nishinaga/Science Photo Library; p. 14 Otto Rogge/ANT Photo Library ; p. 16 Larry West/Bruce Coleman Inc.; pp. 17, 19, 25 Anne & Jacques Six/Auscape; p. 18 Gusto/Science Photo Library ; p. 24 Andrew Henley/Auscape; pp. 26, 29 Corbis; p. 27 CSIRO.

Cover photograph of a worker bee on a flower reproduced with permission of Wade Hughes/Lochman Transparencies.

Every effort has been made to contact copyright holders of any material reproduced in this book. Any omissions will be rectified in subsequent printings if notice is given to the publisher.

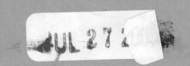

Contents

Any words appearing in bold, **like this,** are explained in the Glossary.

Amazing Bees!

Have you seen bees buzzing around flowers?
Have you wondered what they are doing?
Bees are amazing when you get to know
them close up.

Bees drink sweet **nectar** from flowers. Then
they turn it into honey.

Bees spread **pollen** from flower to flower.
Because of this, plants can grow seeds.

Most bees have black and yellow stripes. Some have red or orange stripes, and others are green, blue, or even red.

What is a bee?

Bees are insects. Insects are animals that have six legs. Insects also have a thin, hard skin called an **exoskeleton** on the outside of the body, instead of bones on the inside of the body.

How many kinds?

There are at least 20,000 different kinds, or **species**, of bees. The biggest bees are about as long as your thumb. The smallest bees are about as big as a sesame seed.

Where Do Bees Live?

Bees live in most parts of the world. They are more often found in warm, wet areas. They do not usually live in very cold places.

Nests underground

Bees make nests to lay their eggs in. Most kinds of bees make their nests underground. Many bees live in burrows, or holes, left behind by rats, mice, or termites. Others dig their own burrows.

This bee is at the entrance to its underground burrow.

Nests above ground

Some kinds of bees make nests above the ground, on a tree branch or wall. Other bees nest in plant stems, or in old stumps and logs. Some bees nest in hollow tree trunks and in spaces between the walls of buildings.

Honeybee nests

Honeybees make the honey we eat. The shelters that honeybees live in are called **hives.** People make hives for honeybees, so beekeepers can collect the honey.

Bees' nests come in many shapes and sizes.

Bee Body Parts

A bee's body has three parts. First is the head, then the **thorax** in the middle, and then the **abdomen** at the end.

The head

On the head are feelers called **antennae**, as well as eyes and mouthparts.

head

antenna

eye

abdomen

thorax

wing

The thorax

The thorax has six legs joined to it, three on each side. Bees have two pairs of wings attached to the thorax.

The abdomen

The bee has a very thin waist between the abdomen and thorax. Many bees have a stinger on the end of the abdomen.

The exoskeleton

The bee's **exoskeleton** covers its whole body. It gives the bee its shape and protects the bee from being hurt easily. It also stops the bee from drying out by trapping water inside its body. The exoskeletons of most bees are covered with hairs.

Shiny bees

Nomada bees do not have many hairs on the exoskeleton. The exoskeleton is usually bright and shiny.

Mouthparts and Eating

Bees eat **nectar** and **pollen**, which are found in flowers.

Making honey

A bee puts its tongue into the middle of a flower and sucks up nectar. The nectar goes into a bag in the bee's body called the honey stomach, where it becomes honey.

Most of the honey comes back out of the bee's mouth later to feed the young and other bees. The bee keeps some honey inside its body for its own food.

tongue

Most bees have a long, thin tongue.

Collecting pollen

Bees use their **jaws** and tongue to bite and scrape pollen from flowers. They carry it back to their nests on hairs on their bodies. Then they mix it with nectar or honey to make a sticky substance called bee bread. They feed bee bread to their young. Bees only eat a little pollen.

Pollen from a flower sticks to a bee's hairy coat.

Eyes and Sensing

A bee has two very large eyes, one on each side of its head. These eyes are made up of hundreds of smaller eyes. This kind of eye is called a **compound** eye.

Bees also have three tiny eyes on the top of the head. These eyes most likely only see dark and light. They probably help the bee when it is flying.

A bee can see all around it with its compound eyes.

Finding their way

Bees can figure out where they are going by seeing where the sun is in the sky. They use the sun as a guide. They also look at trees and other large objects, and use them as guides, too. They are more likely to do this when they already have found food and are going back and forth from the nest.

Bees have three tiny eyes on top of the head.

Sensing the sun

Bees can see where the sun is, even if it is covered with clouds. This is because they can **sense** the sun through the clouds.

13

Antennae and Sensing

A bee has two long **antennae** on its head. It uses them to **sense** things. They are between the eyes and above the mouth. They can be folded back if the bee is in danger, or if it is inside a flower or the nest. This keeps them from being damaged.

Smelling

A bee smells with its antennae. The bee keeps going to the same kind of flower as it flies around. It needs to smell the flowers carefully to do this.

Bees' antennae have a bend in them.

Feeling and hearing

A bee touches things with its antennae. It also feels **vibrations** and hears sounds with its antennae. This helps the bee escape from danger. A bee also feels anything that touches the hairs on its body.

Bees smell and touch flowers with their antennae.

Legs for Moving

Bees' legs have three main parts and a long foot. Bees can walk and run with their legs. They also hold on to flowers with their legs while they are feeding.

The end of the foot has two claws so the bee can hold on to rough surfaces. There is also a pad with hairs on it at the end of the foot. When a bee needs to walk on something smooth, like a window, this foot pad gets sticky.

This bumblebee is gripping a blade of grass with its legs, feet, and claws.

Useful legs

Many bees have hooks on their legs for pulling **wax** off the **abdomen,** where it is made. Some bees have a hook on their front legs for cleaning their **antennae.**

All bees have hairs on their legs for carrying **pollen.** Many bees have pollen baskets on their back legs. These are wide, flat areas with long hairs around them.

pollen basket ←

This bee's pollen basket is full of pollen.

17

Wings and Flying

Bees fly to find food, to escape from enemies, and to start a new nest.

A bee has two pairs of wings. The front wings are larger than the back wings. The wings are clear and very thin. They are held in shape by hard **veins.**

Bees can fly quickly between flowers to find food.

vein

The front and back wings are joined together by a row of tiny hooks. This makes the front and back wings move together.

Flying

Bees beat their wings more than 200 times a second. The beating wings make a buzzing sound. Bees can fly forward, backward, or hover in one place.

A bee folds its wings back over its body when it is not using them.

Clean wings

Bees clean their wings with combs of hair on their back legs.

The Thorax and Abdomen

A bee's **thorax** has wings and legs joined to it. Strong muscles inside the thorax move the legs and make the wings beat fast.

The **abdomen** is made up of sections that look like stripes. Many bees have **wax glands** underneath the abdomen. They use wax to make the **cells** in their nests.

A bee's wings and legs are joined to its thorax.

20

Stingers

Many bees have a stinger on the end of the abdomen. The bee sticks its stinger into an animal, then pumps in a stinging poison. Bees sting animals to teach them to keep away from bees and their nests.

In most bees, the stinger has pointed **barbs** that stop the stinger from coming out. When the bee moves away, the end of the abdomen pulls off and the bee dies.

Biting bees

Meliponini bees do not have a stinger. If an animal upsets their nest, they defend themselves by biting, and they crawl into the animal's hair, eyes, ears, and nose. Some of them pour burning juice onto the animal.

A bee's stinger is a sharp tube on the end of its abdomen.

Inside a Bee

A bee's heart is long and thin. It runs down the middle of the **abdomen.** It pumps blood around the body.

How do bees get air?

A bee has tiny air holes called **spiracles** on the sides of its **thorax** and abdomen. Air goes in these holes and is carried around the inside of the bee through tiny tubes.

What happens to food?

A bee's honey stomach and food stomach are in its abdomen. Most of the honey in the honey stomach comes back out of the mouth to feed other bees in the nest. If the bee needs some food for itself, honey moves from the honey stomach to the food stomach, so the bee can **digest** it.

Waste passes out of the **anus** (just above the stinger) as droppings.

Yellow-faced bees

A yellow-faced bee has very little hair on it. It carries **pollen** in its honey stomach instead of on hairs on its body, like other bees.

heart

food stomach

blood tube

jaw

tongue

honey stomach

pollen basket

anus

Living Together

Most bees live alone. The females usually make the nests underground. The nests have several **cells** in them, each one for a young bee to grow in. These kinds of bees usually live for a few weeks.

Some bees live in large groups called **colonies.** Their nests have many cells, for many young bees. Honeybees have the largest colonies of all, with thousands of bees in them.

A honeybee's nest is made up of thousands of cells that fit neatly together.

Honeybee colony

There is one queen bee in a honeybee colony. She is a large female, and she lays eggs for the colony. She may live for up to five years.

There are some male bees called drone bees. They do not do any work, and live for four months at the most. They may **mate** with a queen bee.

The worker bees are females that look after the queen, the nest, and the young bees. They leave the nest to get food for the colony. They live for a few weeks.

This queen honeybee is surrounded by worker bees.

Life Cycle of Bees

A female bee becomes a mother after she **mates** with a male bee. Bees usually mate while they are flying. The male bee dies soon after.

A mother bee lays her eggs in her nest. One egg goes into each cell in the nest. Then the eggs hatch into **larvae.** The larvae have no legs.

Growing up

The larvae grow in their cells. Some kinds of bee larvae eat food such as honey and **pollen** left for them in their cells. Other kinds are fed by the workers.

A mother bee lays an egg in each cell.

After about six days, the larvae stop eating and moving, and become **pupae** for about twelve days. This is when they change from larvae into adult bees.

Where does a mother bee go?

In most kinds of bees, the mother bee does not stay in the nest. The young adults also leave the nest. These kinds of bees live alone.

In this nest, the worker bees feed the larvae in their cells.

Bees and Us

People keep honeybees so they can collect the honey. The honeybees live in **hives,** which are looked after by a beekeeper. The honeybees make rows of **wax cells** in the hive. They fill them with honey, to store for later, as food for themselves and their **larvae.** The beekeeper takes the cells out of the hive and removes some of the honey. The bees are not harmed when the honey is collected.

Beekeepers wear protective clothing when they tend bee hives.

People use honey to sweeten foods and drinks.

Bee stings

A bee sting can be very painful. Some people can get sick if they are stung by a bee. When some bees sting, they leave their stingers behind in the skin. It should be scraped out carefully. If you press it, more poison can go into the skin.

Pollinating crops

Many farmers also keep bees to **pollinate** their **crops.** When there are more bees, more **pollen** can be carried from flower to flower.

Find Out for Yourself

Try to find some bees visiting flowers. You will probably see more bees on a warm day. Watch as they crawl around on a flower. How long do they stay on each flower? Be careful not to get too close, as you do not want to get stung.

Books to read

Claybourne, Anna. *Insects*. Chicago: Raintree, 2002.

Houghton, Gillian. *Bee*. New York: Rosen, 2004.

Landau, Elaine. *Killer Bees*. Berkeley Heights, N.J.: Enslow Publishers, 2003.

McDonald, Mary Ann. *Bees*. Eden Prairie, Minn.: Child's World, 2003.

Spilsbury, Louise and Richard Spilsbury. *A Colony of Bees*. Chicago: Heinemann Library, 2004.

Spilsbury, Louise and Richard Spilsbury. *The Life Cycle of Insects*. Chicago: Heinemann Library, 2003.

Using the Internet

Explore the Internet to find out more about bees. Have an adult help you use a search engine. Type in a keyword such as *bees* or the name of a particular bee.

Glossary

abdomen   last of the three main sections of an insect

antenna   (plural: antennae) feeler on an insect's head

anus   hole in the abdomen through which droppings pass

barb   curving end of the stinger

cell   small container, like a small room; each bee larva grows in its own cell

colony   group of many insects of the same kind living together

compound   made up of smaller parts

crop   plants grown by farmers

digest   break down food so an animal can use it for energy and growth

exoskeleton   hard outside skin of an insect

gland   body part that makes something for a special use, such as wax or a poison

hive   shelter that bees make their nests in

jaw   hard mouthpart used for biting and holding food

larva   (plural: larvae) young stage of many insects, a grub

mate   when a male and a female come together to produce young

nectar   sweet juice inside flowers

palp   small body part like a finger, near an insect's mouth

pollen   substance on flowers made of dry, dusty grains, usually yellow; plants use pollen to reproduce

pollinate   take pollen from one plant to another, so the plants can make seeds

pupa   (plural: pupae) stage of an insect's life, when it changes from a larva to an adult

sense   how an animal knows what is going on around it, such as by hearing, seeing, or smelling

species   type or kind of animal; animals of the same species can produce young together

spiracle   tiny air hole on an insect's body

thorax   chest part of an insect

vein   small tube in the body that carries blood; dry veins in insect wings are empty

vibration   fast, shaking movement

wax   firm but soft substance

Index